D0618171

CREATING SAND BEACHES WITH POOP

Anita Louise McCormick

Enslow Publishing
101 W. 23rd Street
Suite 240
New York, NY 10011
USA

enslow.com

Words to Know

algae Simple plant-like organisms that make food from sunlight but do not have leaves, roots, or stems.

coral bleaching Coral that has become white because the algae that once lived inside it has died. Global warming is a major cause.

coral polyp A tiny animal that is related to jellyfish and can live as a single creature or in large colonies.

coral reef Living organisms that are made up of polyps and algae. Coral reefs live in tropical and semitropical oceans.

ecosystem The plants, animals, and other organisms that live in an area and interact with each other.

erosion The process of land or beaches being worn down by natural forces, such as wind, water, or ice.

nutrient Any substance that provides nourishment for plants or animals.

sandbar An offshore ridge of sand that can be under or partially above the water level.

sand dunes Ridges or hills of sand that are created by the wind blowing sand into piles.

storm waves Powerful ocean waves that are driven by strong winds of hurricanes and other storms.

Contents

Beautiful White Fish Poop

Imagine you are visiting a beautiful beach in the tropics. The blue sky touches the ocean, and white sand stretches as far as you can see. It's a great place to visit and play. You might take a walk, collect seashells, build a sand castle, or play with a beach ball.

But have you ever wondered what beautiful white sandy beaches are made of? In some parts of the world, sand is composed of many things, such as fragments of rock and shells.

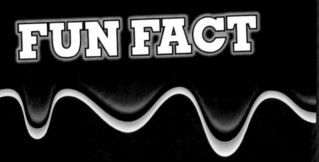

FUN FACT

A single parrot fish can poop an average of 840 pounds of sand per year!

Parrot fish come in many different sizes and colors. This greenthroat parrot fish lives in the Red Sea, near Sudan, Africa.

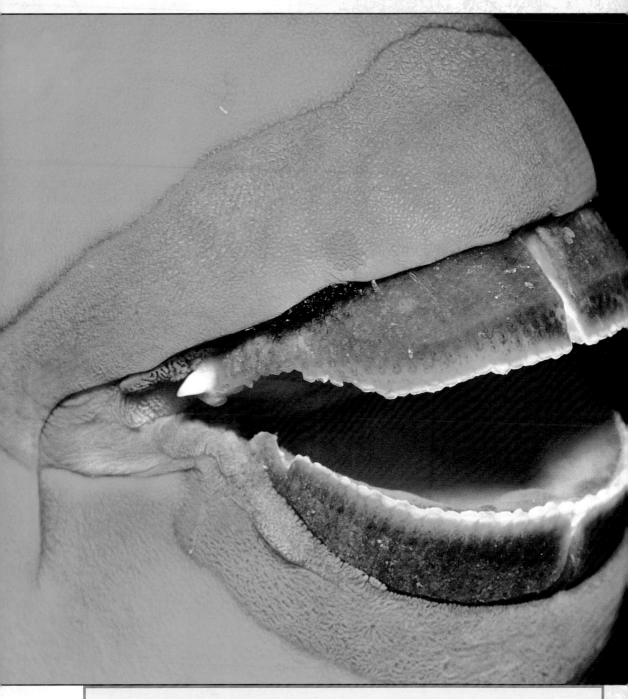

Parrot fish mouths are not only colorful but can also break hard coral into bite-sized pieces. This is a smile that helps create beautiful beaches.

But the lovely white sand on tropical and semitropical beaches is made up almost entirely of fish poop!

While many ocean animals contribute, parrot fish are by far the most prolific sand poopers. Scientists estimate that tropical and semitropical beaches are made of more than 70 percent parrot fish poop!

Parrot fish get their name not only because of their bright parrot-like colors but also because they have large front teeth that are fused together and resemble a bird's beak. This "beak" is strong enough to bite pieces of hard coral so they can eat the algae that grow on it. Their digestive system grinds the coral into tiny pieces. Then parrot fish poop out streams of beautiful white sand as they swim away in search of their next meal.

What Kind of Fish Poops Sand?

The ocean is filled with many kinds of fish. Some fish are so tiny that you can barely see them. Other fish are very large. All fish eat, digest their food, and poop whatever they can't digest into the ocean. But only parrot fish are known for pooping sand!

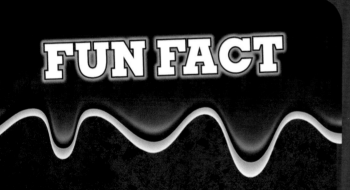

FUN FACT

Parrot fish get their name for their "beak," the visible teeth they use to crunch coral.

Worldwide, there are more than 60 species of parrot fish. The smaller members of the species grow to about 12 inches long, but the largest can grow up to four feet. Parrot fish

Parrot fish enjoy a meal of coral. Before long, they will digest the algae it contains and poop out streams of sand.

live in coral reefs. They can be found chomping coral in tropical and semitropical waters around the world, including the Hawaiian coral reefs, Australia's Great Barrier Reef, and the Caribbean coral reefs.

A bumphead parrot fish develops a lump on top of its head when it becomes an adult. The bump helps it break up coral.

Most parrot fish are very colorful. But some kinds of parrot fish are not brightly colored at all. Bumphead parrot fish, also known as humphead parrot fish, are a dark greenish gray.

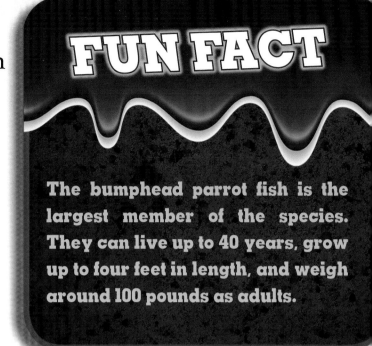

Adult bumphead parrot fish have a big lump on the front of their head. They use this lump to ram into coral, which breaks it into smaller pieces that are easier to eat.

Some people might not think that bumphead parrot fish—swimming through the ocean with huge teeth, a big lump on their head, and banging into coral reefs—are very attractive. But they poop out more beautiful sand per year that than any creature in the ocean!

Biting Off Coral, Pooping Sand

Crunch, crunch, crunch! When scuba divers in tropical and semitropical waters hear that sound, they can be sure parrot fish are nearby.

Parrot fish always seem to be crunching. They love to crunch coral. They do it all day long.

Parrot fish are equipped with a unique set of teeth and a digestive system that allows them to eat coral. Their big front teeth that do all the

FUN FACT

A parrot fish's teeth never stop growing!

These Singapore parrot fish are enjoying a meal together. Like many fish, parrot fish live and eat in communities.

A parrot fish poops out the remains of a meal of coral and algae. Soon the fish will look for more coral to crunch.

crunching are very strong. But that is only the beginning!

Most fish only have teeth inside their mouth. But parrot fish also have rows of sharp teeth inside their throat, which they use to grind up coral. Once the hard surface of the coral has been broken down, parrot fish are able to digest the algae that grow on the coral.

The coral travels through a parrot fish's digestive system and is broken down into smaller and smaller pieces until it becomes the fine sand you may know from beaches. When the coral reaches that point, it's time for the parrot fish to poop!

As they swim, parrot fish poop explosive clouds of white sand particles. These particles slosh through the water, and some eventually make their way to the beach.

What Are Coral Reefs?

Some people think coral reefs are plants since they stay in one place. But a coral reef is really a living colony of plants and animals.

Each individual animal in the coral is called a **polyp**. Coral reefs are made up of colonies of hundreds or thousands of polyps. The polyps

FUN FACT

Coral reefs cover only about 1 percent of the ocean floor but are among the world's most diverse and colorful ecosystems.

The Great Barrier Reef, near Queensland, Australia, is home to many kinds of coral, fish, and other ocean creatures.

extract calcium from the environment and use it to create a hard protective shell for the colony. As polyps die, new polyps grow to replace them.

Tiny single-cell algae live inside the coral polyps, and they exchange gas and nutrients that both need to survive. Because the algae need sunlight to live, coral reefs are never more than 150 feet under the surface of the water.

Coral reefs can be found in tropical and semitropical water in places such as Hawaii,

This reef in the Red Sea, near Egypt, is home to many kinds of aquatic life. It provides fish with an ideal environment to eat, breed, and sleep.

Australia, and the Caribbean. Coral are usually colorful because of the algae that live inside of them.

Coral reefs provide a home for many kinds of fish and ocean plants. Fish that make a home in coral reefs do so for many reasons. Coral reefs usually have plenty of plants or smaller fish they can eat. The coral reef and the plants that grow on it also give fish a place to hide from predators and a safe place to sleep.

Algae, as well as larger sea plants, are an important part of the coral reef ecosystem. When too much algae grows on a coral reef, it prevents the algae that lives inside the polyps from receiving enough sun. This can cause the coral reef to become ill and die. When that happens, the coral turns white. This is known as coral bleaching.

That is where parrot fish come into the picture. They eat the excess algae, as well as some of the calcium coating, which they poop out as sand.

Spreading the Poop Around

When parrot fish poop, it is expelled in big explosive clouds of sand.

Usually, the sand drifts onto the bottom of the ocean. There, the ocean waves wash off any remaining organic materials the parrot fish did not digest.

If the waters are calm, the sand might stay close to where the parrot fish pooped for some time. But eventually, as storms and stronger waves come through, the parrot fish poop washes up onto the beach as sand.

By the time pooped sand reaches

FUN FACT

The older a particle of sand is, the rounder it becomes. This is because the ocean waves push particles of sand against each other, which grinds down sharp corners.

Sandbanks in tropical areas are often made up of coral particles that parrot fish have pooped. Large sandbanks take many years of pooping to build.

the shore, it does not smell bad because the water in the ocean has washed off any undigested algae. That is why sand on the beach is so clean and white. Tiny bits of seashells and rocks are also part of the sand that is washed onto the beach.

Over time, the sand parrot fish poop can also build up sandbars or create entire islands. But this process can take many years and requires tons and tons of poop!

Eating, Pooping, and Sleeping in Mucus Bags

If you watched a parrot fish, you would see they eat nearly all the time!

Since their main source of food is tiny algae, parrot fish have to do a lot of coral crunching to find enough food to stay healthy. Scientists estimate that parrot fish spend about 90 percent of their waking hours looking for food and eating. All this eating means that

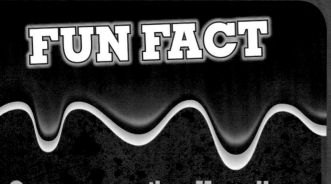

FUN FACT

One name native Hawaiians have for parrot fish translates into "loose bowels."

When parrot fish are ready to sleep, they create a mucus sleeping bag.

These bicolor parrot fish are spawning in a reef near the Revillagigedo Islands, Mexico. Soon another generation of coral crunchers will be born.

parrot fish need to poop out lots of sand so they will have room in their digestive system to eat more tasty pieces of coral!

Like every other animal, parrot fish need sleep. Just like you, parrot fish sleep at night. But before they go to sleep, parrot fish make their own sleeping bags! They do this by belching out a mucus cocoon. This helps protect parrot fish from predators by hiding their scent. It also protects them from parasites that could make them ill.

Parrot fish spend their entire life cycle in coral reefs. They use the shallow waters of coral reefs as a breeding area. The females lay thousands of eggs, then the males come to fertilize them. When they are born, parrot fish have both male and female reproductive organs. Most parrot fish live as female, but during their lifetime, some parrot fish change from female into male.

Who Else Is Pooping Sand?

While parrot fish poop most of the sand found on beautiful white beaches, other ocean creatures also contribute. Sea worms are one kind of scavenger creature that poops sand. They consume mud so they can digest the tiny organisms living inside. They poop out sand and other particles that their digestive system cannot absorb.

Other creatures that poop sand are plant eaters. While they are eating, pieces of coral and seashells are also

FUN FACT

According to Animal Planet, an adult sea cucumber can eat over 300 pounds of poop and animal remains every year.

Spike-covered sea urchins do their part in creating sand and providing nutrients for nearby organisms.

consumed. By the time they are ready to poop, these pieces are ground into tiny bits of sand that can eventually wash upon the beach. Sea urchins are prickly looking creatures that eat mostly sea plants, such as algae and kelp. As they eat these

As they crawl along the ocean floor, sea cucumbers leave a trail of nutrient-rich poop behind them.

plants, they also take in pieces of coral, rock, and shells, which they grind up and poop out. When sea urchins poop, they also release many important nutrients into the ecosystem.

Sea cucumbers also play an important role in this cycle. They move across the ocean floor like vacuum cleaners, eating poop left by other animals, as well as the remains of dead creatures. In the process, sea cucumbers also eat lots of sand. When they poop, they redistribute sand and nutrients. This helps decompose the poop of other creatures before it can cause an overgrowth of algae, which would damage the coral reef. Sea cucumber poop is an important source of fertilizer for seaweeds and sea grass that grows on coral reefs.

Sea cucumber poop is vital to the health of the coral reef. Because sea cucumbers consume so much sand when they eat, their poop is rich in particles of calcium carbonate, a mineral the coral reef needs to repair its outer skeleton, which is constantly being eroded by their environment. The calcium carbonate sea cucumbers poop also helps coral reefs by neutralizing any acid that may be present in the water.

Fighting Beach Erosion

Every time an ocean wave hits the beach, it moves sand around. Some sand is washed onto the beach as more is washed back into the ocean. Wind moves sand from one place to another and creates **sand dunes**.

When more sand is constantly being swept from the beach than ocean waves can replace, it is called beach **erosion**. A major cause of beach erosion is **storm waves**.

Parrot fish poop is one of the most important sources of new white sand.

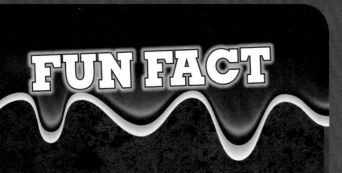

FUN FACT

Healthy coral reefs help protect beaches from erosion by slowing ocean waves before they reach the shore.

Learn More

Books

Brannon, Cecelia H. *A Look at Sand, Silt, and Mud (Rock Cycle)*. New York, NY: Enslow, 2016.

Medina, Nico. *Where Is the Great Barrier Reef?* New York, NY: Grosset & Dunlap, 2016.

Simon, Seymour. *Coral Reefs.* New York, NY: HarperCollins, 2013

Wilsdon, Christina. *Ultimate Oceanpedia: The Most Complete Ocean Reference Ever (National Geographic Kids)*. Washington, DC: National Geographic, 2016.

Websites

Monterey Bay Aquarium, "Parrotfish on Exhibit"
http://www.montereybayaquarium.org/animal-guide/fishes/parrotfish
Meet the parrot fish at the Monterey Bay Aquarium!

Science Kids, "Fun Beach Facts for Kids"
http://www.sciencekids.co.nz/sciencefacts/earth/beaches.html
Learn how sand is made and how the ocean affects it.

World Biomes, "Coral Reefs"
kids.nceas.ucsb.edu/biomes/coralreef.html
Explore the diverse ecosystems of coral reefs.

Index

Published in 2018 by Enslow Publishing, LLC.
101 W. 23rd Street, Suite 240, New York, NY 10011

Library of Congress Cataloging-in-Publication Data

Names: McCormick, Anita Louise, author.
Title: Creating sand beaches with poop / Anita Louise
McCormick.
Description: New York, NY : Enslow Publishing, 2018.
| Series: The power of poop | Includes bibliographical
references and index. | Audience: Grade 3 to 5.
Identifiers: LCCN 2017020674 | ISBN 9780766091061
(library bound) | ISBN 9780766091047 (pbk.) | ISBN
9780766091054 (6 pack)
Subjects: LCSH: Beaches—Miscellanea—Juvenile literature. |
Fishes—Feces—Miscellanea—Juvenile literature.
Classification: LCC GB453 .M43 2018 | DDC 551.45/7—dc23
LC record available at https://lccn.loc.gov/2017020674

Printed in the United States of America

To Our Readers: We have done our best to make sure all
websites in this book were active and appropriate when we
went to press. However, the author and the publisher have
no control over and assume no liability for the material
available on those websites or on any websites they may link
to. Any comments or suggestions can be sent by email to
customerservice@enslow.com.

Photo Credits: Cover © iStockphoto.com/Rostislavv; pp. 5,
6–7, 10, 14–15, 18 ullstein bild/Getty Images; p. 9 Matthew
Banks/Alamy Stock Photo; p. 13 Steve Bloom Images
/Alamy Stock Photo; p. 17 Auscape/Universal Images Group
/Getty Images; p. 21 Thales Paiva/Art in All of Us/Corbis
News/Getty Images; p. 23 Wild Horizon/Universal Images
Group/Getty Images; pp. 24–25 WaterFrame/Alamy Stock
Photo; p. 27 Peter Bischoff/PB Archive/Getty Images; p. 28
De Agostini Picture Library/Getty Images; pp. 31, 32, back
cover (background), interior pages inset boxes (bottom)
jessicahyde/Shutterstock.com; remaining interior pages
(background) Nik Merkulov/Shutterstock.com; interior pages
inset boxes (top) Reamolko/Shutterstock.com.